SOLUTION TO ALL PROBLEMS

YOU CAN SOLVE ALL YOUR PROBLEMS

SUJAL KUMAR SAHA

Made with ♥ on the Notion Press Platform
www.notionpress.com

Contents

CHAPTER ONE

Root Cause of All Problems :

Till 2002 I had been getting success in all of my efforts. I used to stood first from class seven to ten. My rank in West Bengal Joint Entrance Examination for Engineering was 26 and in the same year I was selected for B. Stat. (Hons.) in INDIAN STATISTICAL INSTITUTE, Kolkata. In 2002 my GATE percentile was 98.41 without taking any preparation for that. But in job although I used to finish my coding in shortest possible time my success was not as per my expectations or as per my standard. Initially I used to think others are judging me wrong way. But still I was searching the complete solution.

Then I come to know that there are few major negative emotions which are stopping our progress . Those are Fear (worries tension) , Anger , Pride, Hate, Resentment, Guilt feeling, Criticism, Revenge, Jealousy, Greediness, Superstition.

If you have fear then you can not have confidence , you can not speak confidently or take decision confidently. If you fear from something for long duration or if you fear continuously that something unpleasant would happen then be sure that it will happen in your life. But if you remove fear worries tension from you completely then those unpleasant events will not happen.If you have fear worries tension about your future then your future will not be bright. If you don't fear about your future then I give you 100 % guarantee that there will be no recession on this earth. If you fear about your future then you will not be able to spend your money and then business person will not be able to earn money. All businesses will be greatly affected. So automatically economy will become weak. Then there will be recession on this earth. Economy will be strong only when money will be circulated properly. And to circulate the money you must remove fear.

If you fear from disease then there is high chance that you will fall sick.

Most of the people have anger. Some expresses their anger and some have anger in suppressed state inside them.

In both cases you can not enjoy your life. Goutam Buddha said if you are angry with someone it is like you are trying to throw burning coal towards that person by your hand. So you can understand that your hand will be burnt first by that coal. Other people may be burnt or may not be .

If you have any of these emotions then you can not have peace and happiness always. You must remove them completely to have peace and happiness in your life. You must remove them to have good family relationship and to have brighter future. All problems can be solved if you remove those negative emotions.

I had been searching for long how to remove those negative emotions and now I have come to know easy technique to remove those negative emotions completely. I know most of the people are suffering from one or many of those negative emotions knowingly (consciously) or unknowingly (Unconsciously) . So if you want to have lasting peace and happiness, if you want to avoid recession then you must remove them from your life .

We all have one or many of those negative emotions. But no need to shame because you have not created them yourself. We have got them from the society from our previous generation. So we all are affected by them and playing the role of carrier. So we have to stop here. We will remove them from us and we will not pass them to our next generation.

All problems are in the mind of people only that's why they see the problem in their life also. Once you learn to dissolve the problem from your inner state then the problem will suddenly disappear from your life. "As Within so Without" means "As Inside so Outside". You can change outside events , interaction with people and experiences by changing only your inside. No need to work hard to solve your problems.

Many people are so busy because they are working in their external world all the time . They work hard to meet their need and to solve their problems. They don't know the existence of their inner world . If they work in their inner world for some time everyday then they don't need to work hard to solve their problems. They will be guided to do only those work which will give maximum result.

CHAPTER TWO

Finding Root Cause of the Problem :

If you tell me any of your problem or any problem on this Earth then I can explain to you the root cause of the problem . Most of the cases the problem itself is not at all a problem . The actual cause is completely different and once you resolve the actual cause then you will see there is no problem at all . The problem suddenly disappear automatically. Some examples are explained below :

If one student is not getting good results in exams or not able to build Bright Career then you will say the cause is the student is not talented. But if you analyse the actual cause then you will see the root cause is one or many of the negative emotions.

If you are sick you will say the cause is either germs or bad weather or your body is not able to fight or your old age. But the root cause of all Sickness is negative emotions. One reason could be you feared for long that you will get sick so you became sick or because of negative emotions in you Energy could not flow through all organs of your body freely so that organ could not function properly so you feel sick in that organ.

If you are poor you will think the cause is your bank balance is low or you will say you didn't get opportunity to earn money. Or you will think the environment in which you live is the cause of your poverty. But those are not the actual cause. The root cause is those negative emotions.

If you have enough money but still if you are not able to spend your money then the root cause is negative emotion named Fear.

If you want to start your own business but you don't have money to start then you will say the cause is not having enough money. But the actual cause is the negative emotions in you which is stopping you to start. At this age you can do business with zero bank balance also.

When parents are going for parent child Counselling parents think the problem is in the child only . But the actual cause is the negative emotions in parents or in the maid who look after the child. Because child gets influenced by them and get those problems from them.

If you are getting angry while interacting with one person then you will say the cause is, the other person is not good or he is behaving badly. But the root cause is negative emotions in you. You get angry very easily and it might have formed habit in you.

If you are earning money in dishonest way, by theft or robbery or by taking donations from others or by cheating others then also the root causes are negative emotions named Fear and Greed .

If there is war between two countries or fight between two persons then also the root causes are negative emotions named Anger, Revenge and or Greed.

If you are not confident, not able to speak Confidently, not good in Spoken English, not able to take decision confidently then also the root cause is Fear. If you remove fear you will become confident.

If you are not feeling happy or peaceful all the time then also the root causes are Fear and or Anger.

If you are not able to get good salary , not able to make sales in Business , not getting promotion then also the root causes are negative emotions.

If you are not able to trust others and not able to maintain good relationship with your family members and others then also the root cause is negative emotion.

CHAPTER THREE

How to Avoid Recession?

Recession Cycle
If we remove fear from majority of the people

Strong Economy
To avoid Recession people must remove fear from their mind and the money must be circulated freely.

I know that to avoid Recession and to have Strong Economy we must remove Fear from the majority of the people on this Earth and the money must be circulated freely. I also know easy technique to remove Fear from people. If we remove fear from people then they will not fear to spend money. Then they will buy more goods and services. Then sales will be increased and all companies will make more profit. Then companies will recruit more employees. Then people will earn more money and they will have more to spend. So economy will become stronger.

CHAPTER FOUR

Solution :

In 2007 I learnt prayer from church and by prayer I could solve few problems. Although few prayers were answered but soon I saw some prayers were remaining unanswered for long duration. So after some progress I was not progressing any more. So I needed better solution.

Then I come to know that if we pray with fear, worries, doubt then prayer will not be answered. If we pray with faith, confidence then the prayer will be answered soon . Still I was not able to pray without fear. So I needed some technique to remove fear.

Then I learnt few techniques which helped me a lot. Those are :

Gratitude List : Write down 10 things everyday for which you are grateful.

Affirmation : Repeat few affirmative sentences in your mind . For example "I am happy , peaceful , successful." , "I am grateful for this life" .

Power Life Script : Write down the lifestyle you want in future , record it and listen to it whenever you have time.

Visualisation : Close your eyes and try to make images of your desired lifestyle. See yourself already doing those things now .

Above mentioned techniques helped me a lot but in some situations those couldn't change my feelings. Those techniques couldn't create Energy in me immediately. Those were time consuming. So I wanted to have some easier and faster technique.

Then I learn this method. This is similar to meditation . Here you have to close your eyes , quieten your mind , focus inside and stay there for more than 5 minutes. In this state do not think anything. Even if any thought is coming don't give importance to it , don't try to remove the thought and don't try to hold the thought also . After some time the thought will leave automatically. You will stay as observer. After 5-10 minutes you will start feeling peace and focus on that feeling. If you practice this2-3 times or more everyday then negative emotions will be removed from your mind automatically. If you don't feel peace or don't get result you can send me email to SujalSaha@gmail.com with the book name on the subject of this email. You can practice it alone also but if two or more people practice it together then power will be stronger and the result will be very fast. I have already started building a community where members wants to be healthy, wealthy, happy and peaceful, who wants to help each other , who wants better and advanced life where there will be complete freedom , freedom from all bondage mental or physical. You can join our community and refer your family members, relatives, friends and colleagues and we all can practice it together.

Although mind is very powerful tool it is not unlimited, it has limitation. So you should use mind as a tool only When you need it. Rest of the time you must not use mind , you must not think. When you are doing some project planning or activity planning or doing some mathematics or studying then only use your mind, then only thinking will help you. Rest of the day try to stay mindless or thoughtless. If you use mind or thinking too much then mind will drive you . But actually you should drive mind. You have to learn when to use mind and when no to use.

If you are sick and not able to focus inside or not feeling to apply above methods then repeat few affirmative sentences like "Infinite Energy Heals me" , "I am Grateful for my perfect Health". After sometime you will feel better.

Another method to overcome disease is close your eyes and focus on the organs or place of the body (for example lungs in case of cold cough)which is not functioning properly then say repeatedly "Infinite Energy Heals my lungs" or "I am Grateful for my perfect lungs"

Another method is try to Feel Good. Feeling is very important. If you try to Feel Good always then all problems will be resolved day by day. If you are not feeling good then do something so that you can enjoy your Life. Idea is, you have to enjoy every moments of your life.

CHAPTER FIVE

LEarning Increases Earnings :

To learn we need a certain degree of confidence, not too much and not too little. If we have too little we will think we can't learn; If we have too much we will think we don't have to learn.

If you don't have time to learn new things then follow these steps : write down all your activities, prioritize them, then remove those activities which are not adding any value in your life. Believe me you will have extra hours every day.

If you think you don't have enough money for personal development or you don't want to spend money for learning, let me suggest you one thing , always spend 3% of your income for your personal development or any other training , if you do you will be able to earn more money in future and it will give you a great dividend.

If you think I am happy with whatever I already have, so why should I learn new things then let me suggest one thing . Better is very nice word. You can always try to have better life . You can have all the comforts of life what others are getting but for that you have to develop yourself. Also if you learn new things you will feel happier and more satisfied.

If you think you are now old and you don't need to learn any more then let me tell you one thing . You can not carry your money with you after death but you can carry all your learnings with you forever even after death.

Those who had spent time and money to learn till February 2020 they are not facing any challenges in this situation. Learner will inherit the earth , learner will be well equipped to fight against any situation that may arrive in future.

I spent time and money to understand how to overcome sickness without medicine so now I am not afraid of the current situation. I believe there should not be any disease on this Earth. But it depends on everybody. So it is the responsibility of everybody to make this Earth disease free. I have started my mission to make this Earth free from disease and poverty . I know it is possible but we have to work together . Are you with me in this mission ? Then send Yes to me.

CHAPTER SIX

Change Your Perception and Increase Your Income :

Everything on this Universe depends on your perception . You see this Earth is not moving but actually its moving . when you put a stick in a glass of water you see the stick is bent but actually the stick is not bent. So what you see in many cases are not correct. When you change your perception you will see many situations and many things are changed in your life.

Two man invested all their money in a business and lost everything. One man could not tolerate this loss got sick and remain poor with guilt and resentment. But the other man did not stop trying . He used his knowledge and experience gained from the previous business and earned some money and again started business and then he become wealthy. You see the two man's perception about the same situation was different.

A man was very poor but suddenly he met with a bank manager and he come to know that his father has kept lots of money for him in different account. He used to think he is poor but that was appearance . Similar way many of you may think that you are poor but when you change your perception when you change your beliefs and programming in your mind, you will understand that God , your Heavenly Father has kept lots of wealth for you in the bank of this Universe.

Many of you think you are poor but believe me nobody is poor. once you change your perception and increase your level of awareness and consciousness you will see that you are not poor and from that moment you will start getting wealth.

Many of you see there are many diseases on this Earth but actually all these diseases are created in our environment because majority of people thought disease in their mind first. Once we change our perception once majority of people remove disease from their mind then this Earth will become free from all diseases then everybody can live without any sicknesses.

When this earth will become free from all diseases and poverty (poverty is also one kind of sickness in your mind) then you will feel this Earth has become Heaven. You will feel this Earth is very beautiful place to live in. My mission is to make this Earth a beautiful place to live in and I know it is possible.

CHAPTER SEVEN

How to overcome Sickness ?

I have been applying these techniques successfully since 2007 and from 2007 to 2014 I took medicines only for 3-4 times and since 2015 I never took any medicine. If you follow what I teach , you also don't need to take medicine.

First of all we need to remember there should not be any disease on this Earth. Nature does not create any disease. All diseases are created in our mind first then it's created in our body and environment.

If we can remove our disease from our mind then we will not have any disease in our body.

Eternal truth is that there is only Health in this Universe. By default everybody should be strong and well if he/she believes this.

In most of the cases sickness is a feeling because you feel sick. So if you can replace that feeling with some good feeling then you will not feel sick. But if the feeling is coming from some part of body repeatedly then you must follow the same technique repeatedly. Then after few days that part of the body will recover automatically . The way when we cut our skin it repairs automatically.

How we get sick : There are two functioning in our mind, in one function we understand what we are thinking and in another function (which is called emotional mind) we don't understand what are we thinking in that part . It works automatically depending upon our wrong belief or conviction. In part one if you think repeatedly that you may get sick there is a high chance that you will get sick . But for some people they don't think that they will get sick but still they may get sick suddenly if in his emotional mind one belief is written that "it is normal to be sick" . Now we need to know how this wrong belief was written in our mind . One way is we got that belief from our parents and their ancestors through their DNA or chromosome or gene . Another way is when we are infant or child we don't have power to accept or reject others opinion so whatever comes in our mind through five senses are accepted and are written in our emotional mind. And when we are young even if we have ability to accept or reject but if we accept others opinion as true then also it can be written in our emotional mind . So in these way wrong beliefs are written in our emotional mind and it works in our body according to the nature of that belief without letting us know and suddenly we get sick. This wrong belief written in our mind should be replaced with correct belief then only you can overcome Sickness completely.

Every thought of Sickness first come in our mind then it's created in our body. It may be created in our mind by ourselves or it may come from others. For example some people feel sick when others around them are sick or any of their relative is sick. So some thought of Sickness may be arrived in our mind but not yet created in our body. So sometime we feel sick but doctor does not get any disease in our body because it's still in our mind only, and not yet created in our body. In this case if you only remove that thought from your mind then you can be recovered without medicine.

But if you let this thought of disease remain in your mind sooner or later it will be created in your body . So if you have the disease in your mind and body both then also if you replace that thought and feeling of disease by some good thought and feelings everyday repeatedly then you can be recovered without medicine.

Even if you don't think about disease and if you don't have any false belief you may get sick if you don't remove Fear, Greed, Revenge, Anger, Jealousy, Hatred, Superstition and Criticisms from your life completely. If you have Faith and Love then you will not have above negative emotions. So if you place faith in God and place faith in the belief that There is only Health then you can avoid Sickness easily.

After whole day work you may get pain in legs or hands or in body . Do you know the reason for this pain ? There could be 3 reasons : either your energy is finished or your energy is not distributed to those areas uniformly or blood circulation is not done in those areas sufficiently . If your energy is finished then I am confident you have one wrong Belief in your deeper mind which is "you think that your energy comes from food". But this idea is completely wrong . Because Energy does not come from food Energy comes from God . So you have to learn to get Energy from God then your energy will never be finished because God is the source of unlimited Energy . If you learn to get Energy from God and if you learn to distribute that Energy to every parts of your body then you will never get any pain in any parts of your body. If any organ in your body is not working properly then also it's because Energy distribution and blood circulation are not happening to that organ sufficiently. Energy distribution does not happen properly due to many blockages and wrong beliefs in you which you may not even know that you have. If you learn to remove those blockages and replace those wrong Beliefs with new correct beliefs then you can not be sick .

Most of the people are so much focused on the external things or outside objects and events that they don't even get time to focus inside. So whenever there is even very little problem in any organ of our body they don't understand it at the beginning. So when the problem increases day by day then they suddenly get big problem in any of their body organs. That time problem is big so automatically they understand it and feel uncomfortable and sick . But every human being is given power to understand even very little problem in their organs inside their body. More interesting thing is that every human being is given power to repair his body organs. So if you focus inside every day then you will understand the problems in your body at the beginning of the problem and you can repair it immediately then you will not face big problems inside your body. Whenever any organ in our body does not function properly or perfectly , it gives us signal by pain or uncomfortable feeling . At that time if you take pain killer medicine then the medicine weakens the nerve in that area and so you will not understand the pain. But here we make big mistake. Painkiller medicine or many other medicines do not solve the root cause of the problem. See here your body organ is giving signal that it's not functioning perfectly and instead of repairing that organ you are cutting the signal or you are stopping the signal. But you are actually not solving the root cause of the problem.

Quantum physics says everything is Energy. Einstein said mass is energy suppressed to the point of visibility. So our body is also one form of energy. Every energy has frequency and every energy vibrates. So our body also vibrates. Our body vibrates at different frequency at different times. Our body vibration is registered in our brain as feeling. So our feeling is nothing but body vibration . When we feel sick our body vibrates at low frequency and when we feel ease or comfortable or peaceful our body vibrated at higher frequency . God has given human being only the power to change their body vibration . So we can change our body vibration . And by changing our body vibration we can change our feeling and thus we can overcome sickness.

If somebody speaks very little or if you ask somebody one question and if that person doesn't reply properly or reply in one or two words do you know the reason for this? Let me explain. When we speak we emit sound energy. We know energy neither can be created nor can be destroyed, it can only be converted from one form of energy to another form of energy. So when we speak we actually covert the energy stored in our brain into sound energy. So if a person doesn't have sufficient energy how can he/she will speak lot how will he/she reply to your questions properly. The solution is that person have to learn to increase his/her energy.

If a person is lazy then also its because he/she has less energy. Solution for that person is also same.

If you feel sleepy after having heavy meal at lunch time then it's because your energy used to digest your food so all the energy which was stored in your brain at night is exhausted . So you don't have sufficient energy to operate your body organs so you feel sleepy.

Written on 24.11.2020 :

Nature does not create any disease . All diseases are created in human mind first then it's created in the Nature. Current situation (Covid 19) is also created because majority of the world population thought about disease and sickness. Nature is the reflection of the belief of the majority of the people on this Earth. Majority of the people believe that it is natural to have sickness sometime , it is natural to have disease on this Earth. But if majority of the people would believe on the statement " There should not be any disease on this Earth " or in other way " There is only Health " then the current situation will be improved. So if we can change the belief of majority of the people then we can overcome the current situation. This is the only permanent solution to overcome this kind of situation. Vaccine would protect us from current disease but there would be another disease in future. But the solution which I have written here are permanent . If we can work on

this area there would not be any disease on this Earth . So I have started to help people to change those belief which are

not giving good fruits .If any of you want to change your belief about disease or want to work with me you can contact me . Because together we can improve the current situation.

I spent time and money to understand how to overcome sickness without medicine so now I am not afraid of the current situation. I believe there should not be any disease on this Earth. But it depends on everybody. So it is the responsibility of everybody to make this Earth disease free. I have started my mission to make this Earth free from disease and poverty . I know it is possible but we have to work together . Are you with me in this mission ? Then send Yes to me.

CHAPTER EIGHT

Money is good or bad ?

Some people think having too much money is bad. They think Money is the root cause of all evil or bad work . But it's not correct. Money is not bad thing. Use of money can be either good or bad. If you use your money for wrong purpose then it's bad but if you use your money for good purpose or to have better lifestyle or to build better society then it's good. So earning more money is always good. So never criticize money.Always Love money but not more than human being.

CHAPTER NINE

Build Bright Career :

Want to Build Bright Career ?

You Can tell us What Do You Really Want and We will guide you How to achieve it. If you do what we say your success is guaranteed.

We Have Special Training by Computer Engineer passed from Jadavpur University and trained from America.

After attending this training you will be able to –

- Score Good Result in Exams
- Speak Confidently in Interview
- Improve Computer Skill (Separate Training)
- Improve Communication Skill (Spoken English Separate Training)
- Build Self Confidence
- Get Better Job
- Improve Memory
- Sharpen Your Brain
- Become Creative and Innovative rather than working in competitive mode
- Raise Your Awareness
- Increase Your Energy Level
- Do Big Work in Short time
- Overcome Your Weak Point
- Overcome Fear Worries Tension
- Become Self Reliant
- Remove Anger (Anger Management)
- Manage Stress (Stress Management)
- Overcome Depression (Depression Management)
- Stay Healthy (Strong and Well) (partially from Separate Training)
- Have Better Relationship with others

- Stay Calm in every situation
- Create positive Emotions and good Feelings
- Solve Your Problems
- Enjoy Your Study
- Find out time from your busy schedule (manage your activity , don't try to manage time , time can not be managed. Time is fixed and same for everybody)
- Upgrade Yourself (Personal Grooming , Self Development , Personal Development, Soft Skills)
- Increase Your Wisdom
- Use higher Faculties of Mind (e.g. Perception, Intuition, Reasoning, Willpower....) to achieve what you really want
- We also arrange Industrial Training (Separate Training , if you attend you will get better job easily with higher salary)

Advantages of this Training :

If any student has Fear Worries Tension Anger Guilt Feeling then he can not remember his study easily and can not use his Creative Power and can not Speak Confidently in Job Interviews. But we have easy and proven Technique to overcome Fear Worries Tension Anger Guilt Feeling. So any student whom you know is not at all Brilliant will become brilliant after applying those techniques . After this training student will be able to remember his study easily , he will appear in Exams and interviews Confidently , he will become Creative so he will be able to Solve mathematics or other problems himself , he does not need to study a lot , he does not need to be competitive ,

Many students do not like to study because of some Weak Points in them , but we have easy and proven techniques to overcome all Weak points . Then that student will enjoy study because it will become easy task for them.

We have easy and proven techniques to improve Memory . So after this training students will be able to remember his study easily.

After this training students will understand which Career Path will be good for him , what is his dream and what to target or to which Goal his journey should be.

After this training students will learn to take his Decision himself so he will not be influenced by other people and he will become Self Reliant to build his Bright Career.

Nobody teaches students How to Earn Money . So after completing study a student can think only way to earn money is to get a job. But after this training he will become Creative and Confident so he can earn money by doing his choice business , by providing best Personal Services as I am now providing great services to the society.

Many students have feeling that they can not perform better in their study , but in our training we will help students to increase their Awareness and then he will feel that he can also build Bright Career so then he will enjoy his study .

When I was student I used to feel sleepy after 7 PM . But Now I know it was because I used to be tired easily and tiredness is because of lack of Energy . But in our training we have easy techniques to increase student's Energy . So He will not become tired .

Nature abhors a vacuum . So when a student will be able To remove Fear Worries Tension Anger Guilt Feeling Competitive thought, there will be empty space in them and Nature will fill that empty space with the information of their study and positivity and creativity .

Communication skill does not mean speaking English fluently .It means to use right word at any situation to express his Opinion to others. In this training students will improve Their Communication Skill.

Many students can not speak English only because of Fear. So after this training he will be able to remove Fear so he will Speak English Confidently and if there is no fear they can Communicate their opinion to others easily. I am confident that after attending this training any student can perform well in any exam and interview.

In this training we also train parents to have right attitude towards their children . I have seen many students did not perform well or could not Build Bright Future because parents used wrong words without knowing it's impact on their children. Sometime students could not perform well because parents do not give their children freedom to choose their Subjects which they like most.

If a student has wrong belief or wrong idea about him/her that "he/she can't do this or that" then we have easy and proven techniques to erase that belief or idea from him/her. As long as that belief or idea is fixed in the depth of his/her mind , he/she can't perform well in career.

If a student can stay strong and well always then they can feel more energetic and thus they can easily build Bright Career .

CHAPTER TEN

Increase Your Income :

Do you really want to increase your income ? Do you really want to increase your wealth ?

Law of Increase states that either you are increasing or decreasing . So at this point if you are not trying to increase your income that means you are automatically decreasing your wealth value because of inflation or other factors.

In this training you will learn to increase your income in short duration .

In this training a self employed person or small scale business person will learn to build his own Big Business or expand his existing business.

We Have Special Training by Computer Engineer passed from Jadavpur University and trained from America.

After attending this training you will be able to –

- Speak Confidently
- Improve Communication Skill (Spoken English seperate training)
- Build Self Confidence
- Build a System which will generate income without your intervention
- Build Multiple Sources of Income
- Sell Your Personal Services
- Sell Your Talents
- Sell Your Ideas
- Get Better Job
- Increase Your Wealth
- Improve Memory
- Sharpen Your Brain
- Become Creative and innovative rather than working in competitive mode

- Upgrade Yourself (Personal Grooming , Self Development , Personal Development, Soft skills)
- Enjoy Your Work
- Use higher Faculties like Perception, Intuition, Reasoning, Willpower to increase your wealth
- Raise Your Awareness
- Increase Your Wisdom
- Increase Your Energy Level
- Do Big Work in Short time
- Find out time from your busy schedule (manage your activity , don't try to manage time , time can not be managed. Time is fixed and same for everybody)
- Overcome Your Weak Point
- Solve Your Problems
- Overcome Fear Worries Tension
- Create positive Emotions and good Feelings
- Become Self Reliant
- Remove Anger (Anger Management)
- Stress Management
- Depression Management
- Stay Healthy (Strong and Well) (partially from separate full training)
- Have Better Relationship with others
- Stay Calm in every situation
- Improve Computer Skill (Separate training)

CHAPTER ELEVEN

Increase Your Sales :

Want to Improve Your Business ?

I am working as a Business Improvement Consultant . I get multiple ideas to improve any Business. I will analyze your Business and will give you improvement ideas. You can pay me after you get good results by this idea . If I increase your sales are you ready to pay me for my ideas ?

We Will Help You to –

- Customer Retention
- Increase Your Sales
- Upgrade and Increase Your Business
- Make Your Business Online
- Advertise Your Business
- Build Customer Repository
- Have Multiple Sources of Income

We Have Special Training (by Computer Engineer from Jadavpur University trained from America) To –

- Sell Your Products or Services
- Increase Your Sales
- Build Big Business
- Build Long Term Business Relationship with Customer
- Raise Your Awareness
- Increase Your Energy Level
- Do Big Work in Short time
- Overcome Your Weak Point

- Overcome Fear Worries Tension
- Become Creative
- Use Intuition and Will Power

Advantages of this Training :

When a Business man will be able to remove Fear Worries Or Tension then Customer will feel comfortable to purchase from him . When a Business man will be able to manage his Anger then they can speak with customer with right attitude always and then Customer will come to his shop repeatedly.

In this training a Business man will learn to have long term good relationship with customer and thus it will help them in Customer Retention . Through our website We will also help business man to increase number Of customers and for customer retention .

After this training a Business man can overcome competitive Attitude and will be able to become Creative and can do his Business in a new Creative or Innovative way.

In this training a Business man will come to know what is the right way to do business, what is the right way to earn money or how to earn money without sacrificing Honesty.

In this training you will be able to use Intuition so you will be guided to invest your money in right place and to purchase right shares .

CHAPTER TWELVE

Corporate Training :

We Have Special Training by Computer Engineer passed from Jadavpur University and trained from America.

After attending this training your employees will be able to –

- Goal setting
- Build Self Confidence
- Improve Memory
- Sharpen Your Brain
- Become Creative rather than working in competitive mode
- Upgrade Yourself (Personal Grooming , Self Development , Personal Development, Soft skills)
- Enjoy Your Work
- Use higher Faculties like Perception, Intuition, Reasoning, Will Power to increase your sales
- Raise Your Awareness
- Increase Your Wisdom (Learning Increases Earning)
- Increase Your Energy Level
- Do Big Work in Short time
- Find out time from your busy schedule (manage your activity , don't try to manage time , time can not be managed. Time is fixed and same for everybody)
- Overcome Your Weak Point
- Solve Your Problems
- Overcome Fear Worries Tension
- Create positive Emotions and good Feelings
- Anger Management
- Stress Management
- Depression Management

- Stay Healthy (Strong and Well) (partially from separate full training)
- Have Better Relationship with others
- Stay Calm in every situation
- Improve Communication Skill (Spoken English separate training)

For Senior Citizen :

I have more than 15 years of Spiritual Experience and I attended many trainings from America. I have applied Spiritual Healing technique on me and got good results.I don't take any medicine now .

We Help Senior Citizen to

- Overcome Sickness without Medicine
- Stay Strong till the End of Your life
- Increase Your Energy Level
- Increase Your Awareness
- Get Complete Freedom on this Earth
- Apply Spiritual Mind Healing
- Earn Money even after Retirement
- Improve Your Memory
- Remain Self Reliant even after Retirement
- Remain Active Even After Age 60